READING/WRITING
COMPANION

Mc
Graw
Hill
Education

Cover: Nathan Love, Erwin Madrid

mheducation.com/prek-12

Send all inquiries to:
McGraw-Hill Education
Two Penn Plaza
New York, NY 10121

ISBN: 978-0-07-901865-6
MHID: 0-07-901865-3

Printed in the United States of America.

7 8 9 LMN 23 22 21

C

Welcome to Wonders!

Explore exciting **Literature**, **Science**, and **Social Studies** texts!

★ **READ** about the world around you!

★ **THINK**, **SPEAK**, and **WRITE** about genres!

★ **COLLABORATE** in discussions and inquiry!

★ **EXPRESS** yourself!

my.mheducation.com

Use your student login to read texts and practice phonics, spelling, grammar, and more!

Unit 5 Wonders of Nature

The Big Idea

Week 1 • How Does Your Garden Grow?

SCIENCE

 Digital Tools Find this eBook and other resources at: my.mheducation.com

Week 2 • Trees

SCIENCE

Janette Hill/Alamy

Week 3 • Fresh from the Farm

Unit 5
Wonders of Nature

The Big Idea What kinds of things can you find growing in nature?

 Talk about what you see in the picture. Speak in a loud, clear voice. Use correct grammar, too.

 Circle things that are growing.

Talk About It

Talk about ways these people help their garden grow. Remember to speak in complete sentences as you share your ideas.

 Draw and **write** about one thing plants need to grow.

Plants need

_____

- -

_____

 Retell the realistic fiction story.

 Write about the story.

This story is about

_____

- -

_____

Text Evidence

Page

One thing in the make-believe garden is

_____

- -

_____

_____

- -

_____

Text Evidence

Page

Talk about plants you have seen in a garden.

 Draw and **write** about one of them.

This plant is

_____

- -

_____

Characters are the people or animals in a story. The **setting** is where the story takes place. The **events** are what happen in the story.

 Listen to part of the story.

 Talk about the characters, setting, and events.

 Write about the characters and setting.

The characters are

_____

- -

_____

The setting is

_____

- -

_____

 Draw an event.

Look at the pictures on page 4 and pages 13–17.

 Talk about things in the garden that are real and not real.

 Draw and **label** something real or not real.

Listen to page 24.

 Talk about how the author helps you imagine flowers and strawberries at night.

 Draw and **write** your ideas.

 Make Inferences

What can you tell about the things that the girl grows in her garden? How do you know?

The flowers and strawberries look like

_____

- -

_____

Shared Read

 **Find Text Evidence**

Read to find out what Hop can do.

Underline uppercase letters in the title.

Hop Can Hop!

I am Dot.

I like Hop.

Shared Read

🔍 **Find Text Evidence**

✏️ **Circle** the word **my**.

✏️ **Underline** two words that rhyme on page 19.

I am hot.

See my hat on top!

Hop is hot.

Hop can hop on top.

Shared Read

🔍 **Find Text Evidence**

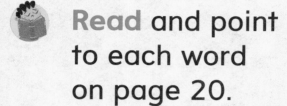

Read and point to each word on page 20.

Circle words that begin with the same sound as **had**.

Hop can hop, hop, hop.

I can hop, hop, hop!

Shared Read

🔍 **Find Text Evidence**

✏️ ◯ **Circle** who can sip.

👥 **Retell** the story. Reread if you do not understand something. Use the pictures to help you.

I can sit.

Hop can sit.

Pop and I can sip.

Hop can sip.

Listen to the poem. Look at the picture. What parts of a plant grow from a seed?

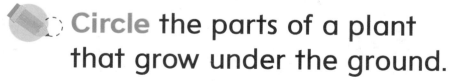 **Circle** the parts of a plant that grow under the ground.

 Draw boxes around the parts that grow above the ground.

Quick Tip

We can talk about plants using these words:

seed, flower, weed, vine, shoot, tree, root

Now talk to a partner about the poem and picture. Use these words.

Listen to the poem again.

 Talk about the rhythm and words in the poem that rhyme.

 Draw a picture of the word that rhymes with **seed**.

 Write About It

Think about the poems you read about seeds and plants.

Write a poem about a plant or a garden.

Parts of a Plant

Step 1 **Talk** about different parts of a plant. Choose a plant part to learn about.

Step 2 **Write** a question about this plant part.

_____

- -

_____

_____

- -

_____

Step 3 **Look** at books or use the Internet. You can use a picture dictionary to look up words you don't know.

Step 4 Draw and write about what you learned.

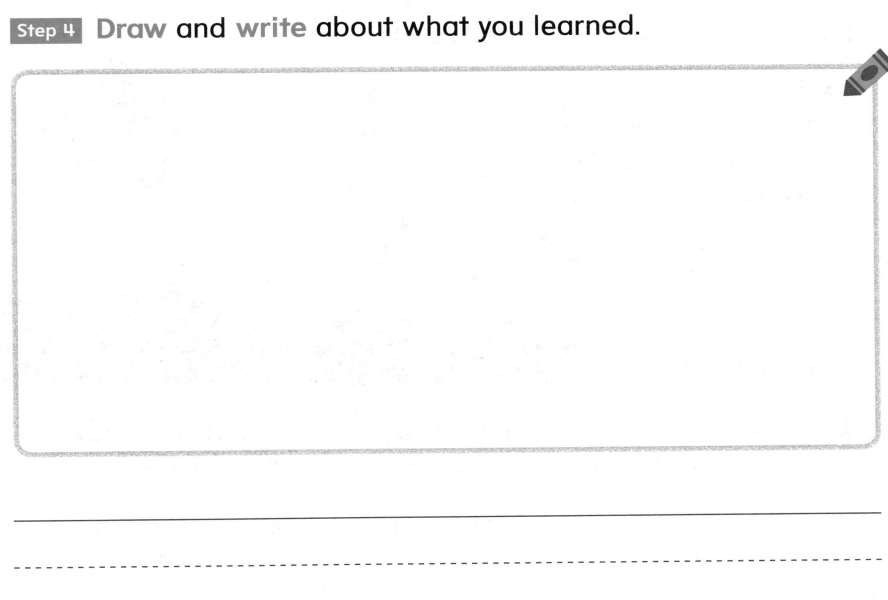

_____

- -

_____

Step 5 Choose a good way to present your work.

Mary, Mary, Quite Contrary

Mary, Mary, quite contrary,
How does your garden grow?
With silver bells and cockle-shells,
And pretty maids all in a row.

 Talk about the things that grow in the nursery rhyme.

 Think about the things that grow in *My Garden*.

 Compare the garden in the nursery rhyme to the one in *My Garden*.

Quick Tip

A **nursery rhyme** is a short poem for children that was written long ago. A nursery rhyme has rhyming words and a rhythm, or a beat.

What I Know Now

Think about the texts you read this week.

The texts tell about
_____

- -

_____

- -

_____

 Think about what you learned this week.
What else would you like to learn?
Talk about your ideas.

 Share one thing you learned about
realistic fiction stories.

Talk About It

Talk about the little tree.
How might it change as it grows?

 Draw how the tree might change
as it grows.

Write about your drawing.

The tree might

_____

- -

_____

Colin Anderson/Photographer's Choice/Getty Images

Retell the nonfiction text.

 Write about the text.

An important fact is

_____

- -

_____

 Text Evidence

Page

The most interesting part is

_____

- -

_____

 Text Evidence

Page

- -

_____

Talk about a tree you have seen.

 Draw and **write** about the tree.

This tree

**The main topic is what a text is mostly about.
Key details give information about the topic.**

 Listen to part of the text.

 Talk about the main topic.

 Write the main topic.

The main topic is

_____

- -

_____

_____

- -

_____

Draw two key details that tell about the main topic.

1.

2.

Listen to part of the text.

 Talk about words the author uses. How does she make the tree seem like a person?

 Write the words.

_____

- -

_____

The tree is like a person because

_____

- -

_____

Look at the shape of the words on page 29. How does the shape help you picture the trees?

 Talk about why the author put the words on the page this way.

 Draw one of the trees.

Find Text Evidence

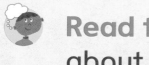 Read to find out about Ed and Ned.

Underline words that begin with the same sound as **egg**.

Ed and Ned

Paul Souders/Photodisc/Getty Images

Ed is not a pet.

Ned is not a pet.

 **Find Text Evidence**

Circle the words that tell where Ned is.

Underline words that have the same middle sound as **hen**.

Ned is up, up, up.

See Ned! See Ned!

Janette Hill/Alamy

Ed met Ned.

Ned met Ed.

🔍 **Find Text Evidence**

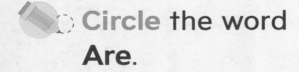 **Underline** words that begin with the same sound as **egg**.

Circle the word **Are**.

Ed can sip, sip, sip.

Ned can sip, sip, sip.

Are Ed and Ned hot?

Are Ed and Ned wet?

 **Find Text Evidence**

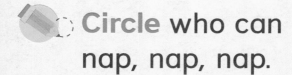 **Circle** who can nap, nap, nap.

Retell the text. Reread if you do not understand something. Use the photos to help you.

Raimund Linke/Photodisc/Getty Images

Ed can hop, hop, hop.

Ned can nap, nap, nap.

a seed   The seed sprouts.   a seedling   a sapling

 Look at the diagram. What can we learn about how apples grow?

 Circle the picture that shows the seed sprout.

 Draw a box around the sapling.

Quick Tip

A **diagram** is a drawing that explains something.

This diagram shows how an apple seed grows into a sapling.

Talk about the diagram. How does it show what a seed needs to sprout?

 Write about two things a seed needs to sprout.

A seed needs

_____

1. _____

_____

2. _____

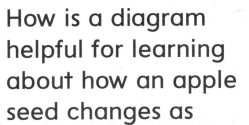

Talk About It

How is a diagram helpful for learning about how an apple seed changes as it grows?

How a Tree Grows

Step 1 **Talk** about how trees change as they grow. Choose one kind of tree to learn about.

Step 2 **Write** a question about your tree's life cycle, or how your tree changes as it grows.

_____

- -

_____

_____

- -

_____

Step 3 **Look** at books or use the Internet.

Step 4 Draw what you learned. Add a label.

My tree is a

Step 5 Choose a good way to present your work.

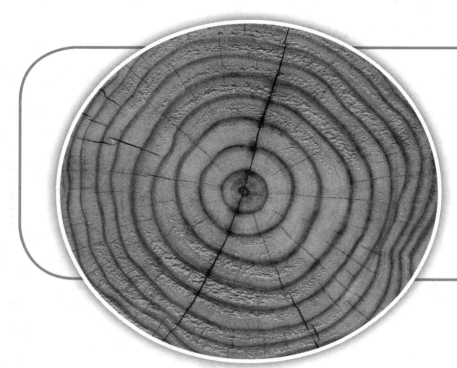

This photo shows **rings**, or circles, in a tree stump.
Some trees grow one ring each year.

 Think about what you can learn from the photo and caption.

 Tell a partner how old you think this tree was.

 Compare what you can learn from this photo to what you read about trees this week.

Quick Tip

Captions tell about what you see in photos and pictures.

Imagemore/Glow Images

What I Know Now

Think about the texts you read this week.

The texts tell about

_____

- -

_____

_____

- -

_____

 Think about what you learned this week.
What else would you like to learn?
Talk about your ideas.

 Share one thing you learned
about nonfiction texts.

Talk About It

Talk about a food you see in the photo.

 Draw and **write** about something you can make with this food.

I can make

_____

- -

_____

Ariel Skelley/Blend Images/ImageSource

Retell the nonfiction text.

 **Write** about the text.

An important fact is

_____

- -

_____

 Text Evidence

Page

The most interesting part is

_____

- -

_____

Text Evidence

Page

- -

_____

Talk about foods in your store that come from farms.

 Draw and **label** one of these foods.

This food is

_____

- -

_____

The **main topic** is what a text is mostly about.
The **key details** give information about
the topic.

 Listen to part of the text.

 Talk about the main topic.

 Write the main topic.

The main topic is

_____

_____

_____

_____

Draw two key details that tell about the main topic.

1.

2.

Talk about how the pictures on pages 20–21 show what the trip was like.

 Draw one place from the trip.

The trip was

Look at the picture on pages 30–31.

 Talk about what other things are "bursting with the seasons inside" like the orange.

 Draw and **label** them.

Find Text Evidence

Read to find out what Ron and Red do.

Circle the word **with**.

Ron With Red

Ron is with Red.

Red is a pet.

Find Text Evidence

Underline the word **He**.

Circle the word that begins with the same sound as **fed**.

Red can see a 🐦.
bird

Can Ron see it on top?

Dad can see ten .
oranges

He can fit ten in a .
basket

Shared Read

🔍 **Find Text Evidence**

⬭ **Circle** words that begin with the same sound as **rat**.

⬭ **Underline** words that tell where the bird is.

Red can see a 🐦.
bird

Can Ron see it on top?

Mom can see ten .
tomatoes

Mom can fit ten on top.

Shared Read

 Find Text Evidence

 Read and point to each word in the sentences on page 67.

Retell the story. Look at the pictures if you do not understand something.

Ron can sit and sip.

Red can see a .

bird

Ron did not see a .
bird

Red can see it on top!

Look at the photos. What do they tell you about ways farmers sell their foods?

Sean Locke/the Agency Collection/Getty Images; Jill Braaten/McGraw-Hill Education

 Circle one way farmers sell foods nearby.

 Draw a box around one way foods travel to places far away.

Quick Tip

We can talk about where places are by using these words:

close, nearby

distant, far away

Talk about ways farmers can sell their foods.

Write about ways farmers can sell their foods.

Farmers sell foods

_____

- -

_____

Farmers sell foods

_____

- -

_____

- -

_____

Talk About It

Look at pages 38–39. How is the information on page 38 different from the information on page 39?

Research a Plant

Step 1 Talk about plants that grow on a farm.
Choose one to learn about.

Step 2 Write a question about the plant.

_____

- -

_____

_____

- -

_____

Step 3 Look at books or use the Internet.
Look up words you do not know.
Use a picture dictionary.

Step 4 Draw and write about what you learned.

I learned

_____

- -

_____

Step 5 Choose a good way to present your work.

Make Connections

 Talk about the farm in the photo. What is special about this farm?

 Compare this farm to the farm in *An Orange in January*.

Quick Tip

To talk about farms, we can say:

The farm in this photo is ____.

The farm in the text is ____.

This community farm grows on a rooftop in the city.

julief514/iStock/Getty Images

What I Know Now

Think about the texts you read this week.

The texts tell about

_____

- -

_____

_____

- -

_____

 Think about what you learned this week.
What else would you like to learn?
Talk about your ideas.

 Share one thing you learned
about nonfiction texts.

My Sound-Spellings

Aa a — apple	**Bb** b — bat	**Cc** c ck k — camel	**Dd** d — dolphin
Ee e — egg	**Ff** f — fire	**Gg** g — guitar	

Hh h_ — hippo	**Ii** i — insect	**Jj** j — jump	**Kk** c k ck — koala
Ll l — lemon	**Mm** m — map	**Nn** n — nest	

Oo o — octopus	**Pp** p — piano	**Qq** qu_ — queen	**Rr** r — rose
Ss s — sun	**Tt** t — turtle	**Uu** u — umbrella	

Vv v — volcano	**Ww** w_ — window	**Xx** x — box	**Yy** y_ — yo-yo
Zz z _s — zipper			

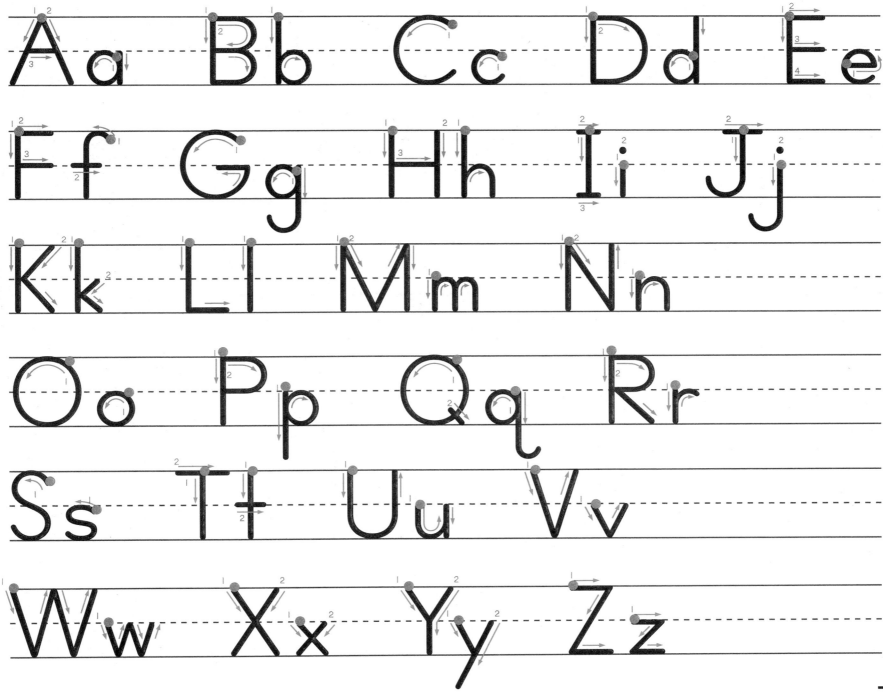